James W Kavanagh

A Reply to Mr. Gladstone's Vaticanism

James W Kavanagh

A Reply to Mr. Gladstone's Vaticanism

ISBN/EAN: 9783743324749

Manufactured in Europe, USA, Canada, Australia, Japa

Cover: Foto ©ninafisch / pixelio.de

Manufactured and distributed by brebook publishing software (www.brebook.com)

James W Kavanagh

A Reply to Mr. Gladstone's Vaticanism

A REPLY

TO

MR. GLADSTONE'S VATICANISM.

A REPLY

TO

MR. GLADSTONE'S VATICANISM.

BY THE
VERY REV. JAMES KAVANAGH, D.D.,
PRESIDENT, COLLEGE, CARLOW.

DUBLIN:
JAMES DUFFY AND SONS,
15 WELLINGTON QUAY,
AND 1A PATERNOSTER ROW, LONDON.
1875.

DUBLIN:
JOHN F. FOWLER, PRINTER,
3 CROW STREET.

CONTENTS.

	Page.
Chapter I.—Introduction	1

Chapter II.—The definition of Papal Infallibility and Papal jurisdiction cannot affect the duty of civil allegiance practically . 6

Chapter III.—The condemnations of the Syllabus rightly understood, must receive the assent of all who sincerely wish to preserve Christian civilization and Christian morality . 19

Chapter IV.—Papal Infallibility is no new doctrine, but is as old as the Papacy itself 36

Chapter V.—The so called breaches with history arise from misconception. In breach No. 1 Mr. Gladstone confounds divine faith with Catholic faith; in breach No. 2 he is not correctly informed on the value of the decrees of the Councils of Constance and Basle 42

Chapter VI.—The Roman Pontiff is not " primus inter pares", but always exercised supreme jurisdiction in the Universal Church 58

Chapter VII.—Obedience to the Pope is not changed by the Vatican Decrees 65

Chapter VIII.—In his charge against the Church of the use of force, Mr. Gladstone has not proved that the word "vis" in the condemned proposition means more than the ecclesiastical punishment of her external court . . . 68

Chapter IX.—The Vatican decrees introduced no flaws in the civil allegiance of Catholics 72

Chapter X.—On the intrinsic nature of Papal Infallibility, Mr. Gladstone is not correctly informed . . . 77

Chapter XI.—Conclusion 82

PREFACE.

My purpose, in the following pages, is to give a popular reply to Mr. Gladstone's *Vaticanism*.

As many of the arguments of the *Expostulation* are introduced in *Vaticanism*, it is impossible to reply to it without repeating the opinions and the arguments of the two great lights of the English Church, who have so ably and so eloquently refuted the charges advanced in Mr. Gladstone's first pamphlet. For this repetition I ask the indulgence of my readers.

A REPLY

TO

MR. GLADSTONE'S VATICANISM.

CHAPTER I.

INTRODUCTION.

The painful controversy raised by Mr. Gladstone, if narrowed to its proper limits, seems to me to admit of a very plain and simple issue.

In its religious aspect the controversy has little significance. The rehearsal of trite objections against Papal Infallibility may amuse an ex-Prime Minister during the recess, and form a pleasing variety in his Homeric studies; but the topic can have little interest for the practical mind of England. Had he been content to ventilate his objections against Catholic doctrine, and to exhibit his dexterity as a controversialist for the admiration of his followers, as Irish Catholics, however much we might regret to see our great champion dragged down to the level of an Exeter Hall platform, we could have easily pardoned him this harmless amusement.

But Mr. Gladstone openly professes that religious controversy is but the secondary purpose of his pamphlets, and that his primary object is to prove that the faith of Catholics, as defined by the Vatican Council, if professed sincerely, is incompatible with the duty of civil allegiance.

Under this aspect the consequences of his conduct are grave indeed. They may largely influence the future of the Catholic subjects of this great empire, and involve a responsibility which no good man would lightly incur. Mr. Gladstone knows the temper of the English people. He is well aware their bigotry but slumbers. He cannot have forgotten the unhappy outburst of intolerance, which another ex-prime minister so senselessly evoked; and prudence, wisdom, and justice, should have restrained him from incurring the grave responsibility of again exposing his Catholic fellow-subjects to the outrages they had then to suffer. True, he says, he assails, not the Catholicity of England, but the Catholicity of Rome, which he so politely calls "Vaticanism". This distinction is but a poor subterfuge, and is not worthy of Mr. Gladstone's candour. He is well aware that the Catholicity of Rome and the Catholicity of England, and of all other national churches which form the great Christian community rightly called the Church of God, are identical;

that they have ever been so, and ever must be so; that Rome is the centre of unity of Christian faith; and that a national church severed from Rome, like the Old Catholics of Germany, is but an unsightly caricature of a Christian church—a headless conventicle, and must soon lose the truth of Christian teaching, and glide into one or other of the many isms which so disfigure the religious unity of England. If there are religious tenets which men are bound to profess, there must be some tribunal of final appeal to test their truth ; and if there are no such tenets, then Christianity has ceased to be a dogmatic religion, and becomes a mere code of moral duty, stript of the obligation of faith, without which it is impossible to please God.

If the authority of the Catholic Church is not the tribunal to test religious truth, there is no such tribunal on earth. Not the Eastern Greek Church, where the final appeal is to the Sultan, nor the Russian Church, where the Czar is virtually the judge of religious controversy, nor the German Churches, which retain scarcely a trace of their Christian character, nor the Church of England, in which Parliament frames, or at least will soon frame, the faith of all pious believers; a heterogeneous assembly, where the character of the dogma will largely depend on the party in power, and will be voted, not by good Church of

England laymen, but by Jews, Papists, Presbyterians, Wesleyans, Irvingites, and Freethinkers.

Mr. Gladstone is very wrath against the authority of the Vatican Council, though if he rejects it, to be consistent he must reject Nicea, and deny the Divinity of the Son of God. He is quite scandalized that Catholics should receive their faith from the Church assembled in council, though he knows it was thus the deposit was guarded from the days of the Apostles to the present.

Mr. Gladstone displays great gifts of eloquence and learning in assailing the religion of his Catholic fellow subjects. Would it not be well if he expended a little of his controversial talent in defending the religion he himself professes, and in showing how a faith resting ultimately on a vote in Parliament, can be a rationabile obsequium mentis? If he would quietly allow his excitement to calm down, and permit the storm of the present controversy to die away, I think he might usefully turn aside from his wanton and unprovoked attacks on the Catholic religion, and devote his leisure hours during the next recess to defend the tottering edifice in which he professes to dwell. If Mr. Gladstone knew the happiness of resting his faith on the authority of the Church of God, he would not hope to detach

Catholics from her communion. If he knew how many doubts and anxieties and dreary uncertainties are silenced by the conviction that we are taught by that Church which Christ the Son of God commissioned to teach, even though he could, he should not wish to disturb the faith of the Catholics of this great empire, of which he was so distinguished a minister.

Mr. Gladstone thinks the doctrine of Papal Infallibility was not definable, and repeats the trite arguments of Janus and the Gallicans in support of his opinion; so did the Arians assert after Nicea, that the doctrine of the divinity of the Son of God was not the revealed doctrine of Christ; so said the followers of Macedonius after Constantinople, that the divinity of the Holy Ghost was a novelty in faith; so spoke the Nestorians after Ephesus, and the Monophysites after Chalcedon; so spoke the Monotholites, and the Iconoclasts, and the enemies of God's Church in every age, as from time to time their impious heresies were condemned in the several general Councils, from Nicea to the Vatican.

CHAPTER II.

THE DEFINITION OF PAPAL INFALLIBILITY AND PAPAL JURISDICTION BY THE VATICAN COUNCIL CANNOT AFFECT THE DUTY OF CIVIL ALLEGIANCE PRACTICALLY.

"THE Vatican Decrees do, in the strictest sense, establish for the Pope a supreme command over loyalty and civil duty" (*Vaticanism*, p. 7). This is Mr. Gladstone's main contention. There is a crucial test of the correctness of the statement which no subtlety can evade. I respectfully submit it for Mr. Gladstone's consideration. The relations between a particular sovereign and his subjects can never be the subject of the exercise of the Papal Infallibility defined in the Vatican Council, therefore the defining power cannot affect the duty of civil allegiance. The Pope can define only revealed truths of faith and abstract principles of moral duty; and as the relations of a particular sovereign to his subjects are necessarily invested with contingent circumstances, they can never become the subject of the exercise of the defining power. It is true the Pope can define the doctrine of St. Paul, or any other revealed doctrine regarding civil allegiance; but so he could before the Council of the Vatican met, and so he could in every age of the Church since the days of St.

Peter. The difference in the manner of defining before and after the Vatican Council has no bearing whatever on the civil allegiance of Catholics. Before the Vatican Council, the dogmatic decrees of the Pope, to become articles of Catholic faith, required the tacit consent of the Church; since the Council this consent is not necessary; but as Catholics received and obeyed the Papal decrees with equal alacrity before the Vatican Council and subsequently, how can the decree of that Council possibly affect their civil allegiance? This is the sole difference of the defining power before and after the Council. I should be glad to hear Mr. Gladstone show how it can have any practical bearing on the duty of civil allegiance.

Whether I believe a defined doctrine sanctioned by the consent of the Church, or believe it on the sole authority of the Pope, independently of that consent, cannot practically affect my individual conduct. If the defined doctrine is the same, it will affect my civil allegiance in the same manner, whether I believe it on the authority of the Pope alone, or believe it on the authority of the Pope sanctioned by the tacit consent of the Church. This truth becomes still more clear when we remember what history proclaims, that in no single instance did the Church reclaim against a dogmatic bull, as, since the Vatican Council, every

Catholic knows she could not. If Mr. Gladstone thinks this reasoning is not conclusive, I respectfully ask him to frame and publish a case in which the definition of Papal Infallibility can practically affect the civil allegiance of Catholic subjects.

Mr. Gladstone also complains that the loyalty which Rome upholds is partial and one-sided; that she preaches loyalty to the subjects of sovereigns who are amenable to her behests, and is ready to foster revolution in the dominions of those who are hostile to her claims of power. This at least is impossible as an exercise of Papal Infallibility. The Pope can define no doctrine which is not abstract and universal. All defined doctrines, therefore, on civil allegiance, must affect the subjects of all sovereigns alike. If the Holy Father descends to particulars, and speaks of the special relations of a particular sovereign to his subjects, he must exercise, not his defining power, but his supreme spiritual jurisdiction.

But perhaps the supreme spiritual jurisdiction of the Pope, as defined by the Vatican Council places in peril the civil allegiance of Catholics. This is Mr. Gladstone's second contention; let us briefly examine its truth. If the supreme spiritual jurisdiction of the Pope as defined in the Vatican Council, and as exercised before the Council, must practically affect the civil allegiance of Catholics in precisely the same manner, Mr. Gladstone, I presume, will admit, that the decrees of the Council afforded him no just pretext for the publications which have made his honoured name so notorious.

This is my contention, and this I proceed to establish.

The definitions of the Vatican Council which regard the supreme jurisdiction of the Holy Father, declare—

1st, That St. Peter was constituted visible head of the Church by our Lord Jesus Christ, and received from Him immediately and directly a primacy not only of honour, but of true and proper jurisdiction over the Universal Church.

2nd, That by divine right, St. Peter shall have a perpetual line of successors in the primacy over the Universal Church, and that the Roman Pontiff is St. Peter's successor in this primacy.

3rd, That the Pope has supreme jurisdiction over the Universal Church in faith, morals, discipline, and government; that he has this jurisdiction in all its plenitude, and that it is ordinary and immediate over all the members of the Church, pastors and people.

To understand clearly this last definition, it is necessary to advert briefly to two Gallican errors which the definition condemns. The Jansenists, with a subtlety peculiarly their own, endeavoured to evade the censures of the Church by torturing her definitions and misrepresenting the plain meaning of her teaching. They did not deny that the Pope had supreme jurisdiction in the Church, knowing that this doctrine could not be reconciled with the teaching of the Council of Trent, but they hoped to evade the force of the decree, and to render the supreme jurisdiction of the Pope nugatory in its exercise, by declaring that it was mediate, and that outside the diocese of Rome, except on extraordinary occasions, it could not be lawfully exercised without the consent of the Bishops. The Council of the Vatican condemned this error, and defined the supreme jurisdiction of the Holy Father to be immediate in the Universal Church; so that it is now de fide catholica, that he has the power to perform in every diocese of the Church all the episcopal functions independently of the will of the several Bishops.

The action of Pius VI. in the French Church proves that the papal jurisdiction was supreme, and was the source and fountain of all jurisdiction in the Church of God. If, then, the Popes, centuries before the Vatican Council met, possessed and exercised the jurisdiction which was there defined, how can the definition possibly affect the duty of civil allegiance?

The second error of the wily Jansenists which was condemned in the Vatican Council was, that the jurisdiction of the Pope, though supreme and universal, was not ordinary—that is, did not arise from his primacy—but was delegated to him by the faithful, to whom it was given by Christ. This error was also advanced in the acts of the famous Synod of Pistoia, and was condemned by Pius VI. in the bull " Auctorem fidei".

The Vatican Council also declared that the Pope has the right of free intercourse with the pastors and people of the whole Church, that his acts do not require the sanction of the civil power, that he is the supreme judge in all ecclesiastical causes, that his is the highest authority in the Church, and that, hence there is no appeal from the decisions of the Pope to a general council, as to an authority higher than that of the Roman Pontiff. Let us now briefly examine the teaching of the Church on Papal jurisdiction before the Vatican Council, and see if the Council introduced any change, and what change, and whether the change introduced could practically affect the civil allegiance of Catholics and justify the injurious suspicions which Mr. Gladstone endeavoured to excite against their loyalty. A brief sketch of the history of Gallicanism is the simplest proof that the jurisdiction which the Popes claimed and exercised in every age of the Church is identical with the jurisdiction defined in the Vatican Council. Gallicanism first appeared when, unhappily, Urban VI. and Clement VII. were rival claimants for the Papal Chair, and in their straits did many things which were not in conformity with ancient discipline. The collation of benefices by the Pope and the imposing of new obligations on benefices, were probably the immediate cause of the effort in France to limit the legitimate authority of the Roman Pontiff. The agitation commenced in the University of Paris, where the distinguished men of the several faculties were chagrined to see the rich benefices which they regarded as the legitimate reward of their learning, conferred on strangers. The agitation thus commenced by the clergy in the reign of Charles VI., was cordially seconded by the civil power. The first document in which the Gallican liberties in their crude form were put forth was a royal edict of Charles VI., dated the 7th of May, 1399, which enacts that the Gallican Church should continue to enjoy for the future the liberty, which, according to the sacred canons, she had from her foundation. We next meet the famous Pragmatic Sanction of Charles VII., which was condemned by Rome, and abrogated by Lewis XI. and

Francis I. On the 19th of March, 1682, was issued the declaration of the Gallican clergy, which (1) denied the indirect temporal power of the Pope; (2) asserted the superiority of the authority of a general council; (3) denied the right of the Pope to dispense the canons of the Universal Church, and (4) taught that dogmatic decrees were not infallible judgments without the tacit consent of the Church. When this document was published there were one hundred and thirty bishops in France. By threats, violence, and promises of court favour, the Grand Monarque induced just thirty-four bishops to affix their names to the document, and yet James Benignus Bossuet published it as the declaration of the whole Gallican clergy. For minute and interesting details of this infamous attempt to limit the jurisdiction of the Holy Father, and to strip him of his infallible authority, see *Dublin Review* for October, 1869.

The declaration of the Gallican clergy was followed on the 3rd of March by a royal edict commanding all the clergy to profess and teach the doctrines of the declaration; and finally Bossuet published his defence of the declaration of the Gallican clergy. So matters remained until the 11th of April, when Innocent XII. condemned the propositions of the Gallican liberties, and received from the bishops who had signed the declaration the following solemn retractation of their errors :—

"Ad pedes sanctitatis vestræ provoluti profitemur ac declaramus nos vehementer et supra id quod dici potest ex corde dolere de rebus gestis in comitiis prædictis quæ sanctitati vestræ et ejusdem prædecessoribus summopere displicuerunt ac proinde quidquid in comitiis circa ecclesiasticam potestatem et pontificiam auctoritatem decretum censeri potuit pro non decreto habemus et habendum esse declaramus".

Louis XIV. also, in his better mind, rescinded his edict sanctioning the Gallican liberties. The unhappy Scipio Ricci made a futile attempt to revive Gallicanism in the synod of Pistoia, but the proceedings of that conventicle were summarily condemned by Pius VI. in the bull "Auctorem fidei".

What, then, is Gallicanism, of which Mr. Gladstone has become the distinguished champion? It was an effort of a few discontented priests deeply tinged with secularism, and longing for the flesh pots of Egypt, to sever the French Church from the authority of the Roman Pontiff, and to subject her to the state in her discipline and doctrine—an effort to found a national church on Mr. Gladstone's favourite model, which would not be an independent society divinely constituted, with legislative, judicial, and coercive rights, but an integral part of the civil state, carrying out her behests, and subject to her authority. Here we meet the first official denial of Papal Infallibility. We see the motives which prompted this pernicious error. It arose from the same motives, and was incorporated in the same document with the declaration which endeavoured to withdraw from the Holy Father the supreme government of national churches, and to strip him of his primacy, of which the defining power is an integral and essential element.

The very same spirit which inspired the framers of the Gallican liberties inspires Mr. Gladstone. He would draw those "fangs" and pare those "claws", to which he so politely alludes, and deprive the Pope of the right of inflicting censures, of publishing rescripts, of granting jubilees, of citing culprits, of sending legates, of regulating dioceses, or calling councils, except as the servant of the civil authority.

Mr. Gladstone unfortunately lives two centuries too late. He would have been a distinguished colleague and efficient ally of Dupin, Febronius, Eybel, Ricci, Sarpi, Tamberini, and Ruher, and of the other advocates of this wicked and pernicious form of Erastianism; but Gallicanism is dead and buried, and all the genius and eloquence of Mr.

Gladstone could not give it one pulsation of spasmodic life. Innocent XII. and Alexander VIII. wrote its epitaph, and Pius VI. sang its requiem. This brief history of Gallicanism affords conclusive evidence, that, centuries before the Vatican Council, the Popes claimed and exercised the supreme, immediate, and ordinary jurisdiction which is now defined. Papal jurisdiction was, at all times, episcopal and immediate in the Universal Church. Of this there is the fullest evidence in Scripture, tradition, and Church history. In Chalcedon Pope Leo is called "Papam aut Ecclesiæ Universalis episcopum". In the letter of the sixth General Council to Pope Agatho, we find, "Itaque tibi ut primæ sedis antistiti Universalis Ecclesiæ quid agendum sit reliquimus". In the Council of Lateran, 649, the pope is called "Toto orbé apostolico universalem pontificem". In 512 the bishops of the east, writing to Pope Symmachus say, "Quotidie a sacro doctore tuo Petro doceris oves Christi per totum habitabilem mundum creditas tibi pascere". In the fourth Council of Lateran, can. V., "Disponente domino supra omnes alias ordinariæ potestatis habere principatum". In Florence, "Traditam esse Romanæ Pontifici in beato Petro plenam potestatem pascendi regendi et gubernandi ecclesiam Universalem". Council of Trent, sess. XIV., cap. VII., " Unde merito pontifices maximi pro suprema potestate sibi in ecclesia universa tradita causas aliquas criminum graviores suo potuerunt peculiari judicio reservare.

It is useless to urge this point farther. The Pope at all times vindicated to himself, and exercised, the identical jurisdiction which was defined in the Vatican Council, and if any theologian or canonist denied that the jurisdiction of the Pope was supreme, immediate, and ordinary, he was summarily condemned.

If therefore the supreme spiritual jurisdiction of the Pope, defined in the Vatican Council, was already recognized in the Church and exercised by the popes, how can its definition affect practically the question of civil allegiance? The words in the decrees of the Vatican Council were introduced to condemn the errors of Jansenists and Gallicans; they define the nature of the jurisdiction, but do not affect its exercise. I doubt if there are a dozen lay Catholics in the Church who understand their bearing and significance. It is not quite clear that Mr. Gladstone himself had these distinctions clearly before his mind when writing, yet he rests his grave charges on distinctions which, I believe, he did not thoroughly comprehend, which, though they affect the theory of papal jurisdiction, have no practical bearing on its exercise in relation to the practical life of Catholics and their duty of civil allegiance. Catholics were as much bound by papal rescripts, and were as ready to obey them, before the Vatican Council as they are now. The Pope had at all times the authority which the Vatican Council defined, to issue bulls, briefs, and rescripts, and to enforce their observance, if necessary, by censures. How can the mere definition of this power affect civil allegiance, or justify Mr. Gladstone's grave charges against the Catholics of these kingdoms? Before the Vatican Council, Mr. Gladstone was quite satisfied with the loyalty of Catholics; nay, he boasts, and justly boasts, that for thirty years he laboured to secure them their civil rights. If the Vatican Decrees cannot possibly introduce any practical change in the duty of civil allegiance under any possible combination of circumstances, how can Mr. Gladstone justify his change of policy and vindicate the justice of the grave charges and injurious suspicions put forth in his recent pamphlets? He has gathered up and flung at us the rubbish of Janus, Quirinus, and their colleagues. He has endeavoured to arouse against us the dormant spirit of bigotry; but so far he has succeeded only in dragging down the highest reputation in Europe, and in associating in the columns of *The Times* his honoured name with that renowned brace of Protestant champions whose antics are so notorious. Few regret this unhappy incident in the life of this great and good man more sincerely than the writer of these pages.

CHAPTER III.

THE CONDEMNATIONS OF THE SYLLABUS, RIGHTLY UNDERSTOOD, MUST RECEIVE THE ASSENT OF ALL WHO SINCERELY WISH TO PRESERVE CHRISTIAN CIVILIZATION AND CHRISTIAN MORALITY.

WHETHER the action of the Papal power in the middle ages, and after the breaking up of the Roman Empire, is the parent of our civilization, is a question totally irrelevant. With medieval society, under certain aspects, I am as little pleased as Mr. Gladstone, and to some of the doings of certain popes and certain prelates, I am not less hostile than the distinguished writer of *Vaticanism*. Medieval society painfully illustrates the evils which result when Church and State are leagued together to oppress the masses, and how sad are the consequences if the Church even partially abandons her proper mission of sanctifying the world, and aspires to the uncongenial function of ruling it. I speak of national churches in which a secular and unapostolic spirit was developed by a too intimate intercourse with the State, and which were saved from lower depths by the action of Papal authority, which enforced the observance of a more strict canonical discipline.

The author of *Vaticanism* is evidently not aware that the condemnation of erroneous propositions is the normal way of proscribing error and teaching truth in the Catholic Church, and writes as if the Syllabus was unique, and as if Pius IX. was the first Pope who had recourse to this method of instructing the faithful. From Leo X. to the present, various Popes from time to time, in bulls, briefs, and rescripts, have condemned about seven hundred propositions, and these condemnations, interpreted by theologians according to strict and well-defined rules, form a vast body of Catholic doctrine. It is unfair to deny to Pius IX. a privilege enjoyed and used by all his predecessors, of condemning propositions in a fixed and determined sense and according to fixed principles. All former Popes possessed the right of condemning erroneous propositions in the sense in which their authors used them, as interpreted by the context. The Jansenists, of whom Mr. Gladstone is an apt pupil, denied this right to the Pope of condemning propositions in the relative sense, and when Innocent X. condemned the five propositions of Jansenius, urged this distinction against the validity of the censure. It is certain that the Church has condemned propositions in the sense which is given to them by the context of the works from which they were extracted, which in their nude sense, and apart from the context, express orthodox doctrine. Take, for example, the proposition extracted from the writings of Huss, and condemned in the fifteenth session of the Council of Constance, " Duæ naturæ divinitas et humanitas sunt unus Christus". Apart from the context of the work of Huss, from which it was taken, this proposition expresses the Catholic doctrine of one person and two natures in Christ, but, as interpreted by the context, it expressed an error, and in that sense only was it condemned.

The Church condemned this proposition of Huss as she condemns all other propositions, and as Pius IX. condemned all the propositions of the Syllabus, namely, in the sense which they have in the books from which they were extracted, as interpreted by the context of the writer.

Mr. Gladstone therefore has no right to take up the propositions of the Syllabus, nudely and apart from the context of the books from which they were extracted, and to found on them charges against the doctrine and discipline of the Catholic

Church; he might as well select the proposition of Huss condemned in the Council of Constance, and infer from it that the Catholic Church condemned the doctrine of two natures and one person in Christ. To reason justly, he should procure the several works from which the propositions of the Syllabus were extracted, carefully determine their meaning as interpreted by the context, take their strict contradictories, as the doctrine asserted under censure, and so reason from them. But he is clearly excited; the style, manner, tone, and language of his pamphlets show this but too plainly. If he allowed himself to think over the matter calmly, he must see how unfair is his present line of argument. For centuries the Church has fixed rules for the interpretation of condemned propositions. These rules are strict, well defined, and certain: they are set forth in numberless Catholic writers, and for centuries have been applied by Catholic theologians in the interpretation of all the propositions ever condemned by the Church. These rules expressly state that all propositions are condemned in the relative sense, and that their strict contradictories only are asserted under censure. What right has Mr. Gladstone to assume that Pius IX. has not acted like his predecessors, and has not condemned the propositions of the Syllabus in the relative sense, but in the crude and absolute sense of the words, independently of the context of the works from which they were extracted?

My contention therefore is, that the propositions of the Syllabus should be interpreted like all other propositions condemned by the Church; and interpreted thus, I challenge Mr. Gladstone to deduce from them any doctrine unworthy of the teaching of a Christian Church, in faith, morals, or discipline. Schreader, the German Jesuit, is no authority, but the Pope complimented him. I presume he deserved the distinction. The Pope complimented Louis Veuillot also. Does Mr. Gladstone expect us to receive the fiery editor of the *Univers* as an exponent of Catholic doctrine? This is really childish.

The first charge against the Holy Father is, that he condemns freedom of worship and liberty of the press. The proposition on which this charge is founded is, I presume, the 79th of the Syllabus, condemned in the allocution, *Nunquam fore*, published December 15th, 1856:—

" Enim vero falsum est civilem cujuscunque cultus libertatem itemque plenam potestatem omnibus attributam quaslibet opiniones cogitationesque palam publiceque manifestandi conducere ad populorum mores animosque facilius corrumpendos ac indifferentismi pestem propagandam".

The Pope condemned this proposition. Will Mr. Gladstone undertake to defend it in the face of the Christian people of England?

The proposition states: "It is false to say the civil liberty of every form of worship whatever conduces more easily to corrupt the morals of the people and to propagate the pest of indifferentism". The Holy Father condemns this statement as false, and this is the sole ground on which Mr. Gladstone founds his famous charge. Will Mr. Gladstone himself refuse his assent to this condemnation rightly understood? Can any sincere believer in revelation refuse his assent to it? Can any one who does not wish to see Christian morality extinguished and Christian civilization extirpated, dissent from the condemnation of this infamous proposition?

The great towns of England are reeking with abominations, the rural districts are seething in ignorance and vice, a spirit of irreligion and of indifference to every form of Christian belief is spreading amongst all classes of society like a dire pestilence. Yet a former minister of this Christian state assails the Holy Father for his mild censure on the infidelity of the age, opens more widely the floodgates of vice, and asserts, in the face of Christian Europe, that the civil liberty of every form of religious worship, Mormonism for example, does not conduce to corrupt the morals of the people, and to spread amongst them a spirit of indifference to every form of religious belief!

The Americans love liberty of speech and freedom of worship under all its forms, yet in word and in act they assent to the Pope's condemnation by driving Mormonism from the state. Will Mr. Gladstone become the champion of the Mormons, and say it is false that the civil liberty of Mormonism tends to corrupt the morals of the people? The Holy Father asserts this and nothing more in the condemnation of the proposition which says : " Falsum ut civilem cujuscumque cultus libertatem conducere ut populorem mores animosque facilius corrumpendos". The second part of the condemned proposition is, " Also it is false to state that the full power granted to all of publishing, openly and publicly, all their opinions and thoughts whatsoever, tends more easily to corrupt the morals of the people and to propagate the pest of indifferentism". The Pope condemns this proposition, and says it is not false to state that the full liberty granted to all of publishing all their opinions and thoughts whatsoever, tends to corrupt the morals of the people. The writer of *Vaticanism* assents to this condemnation, the Legislature and the public opinion of England assent to it, and of this assent the law against immoral publications is the outcome. Mr. Gladstone endeavours to extend the condemnation, but vainly; for, as I have shown, its extent is determined by fixed and well defined principles universally observed in the interpretation of all condemned propositions.

If Mr. Gladstone had calmly ascertained in what sense propositions are condemned, and how the precise extent of the condemnation is determined —if he had quietly analysed the several propositions of which he writes with so much froth and fume, he would never have published against the Holy Father a piece of special pleading unworthy of a fourth-rate village attorney.

The next proposition to which he takes objection is the 19th of the Syllabus, and was condemned in the allocution, "*Singulare quadam*", December 9th, 1854.

"Ecclesia non est vera perfectaque societas plane libera nec pollet suis propribus et constantibus juribus sibi a divino suo fundatore collatis sed civilis potestatis est definire quæ sint Ecclesiæ jura ac limites inter quos eadem jura exercere queat".

I distinctly state, Mr. Gladstone's scholarship notwithstanding, that he should not have translated jura by the words, "civil rights".

The proposition speaks exclusively of ecclesiastical rights, and speaks so clearly and so definitely, that if Mr. Gladstone had read the proposition, he could not possibly have mistaken its meaning. This is another illustration of the reckless manner in which he has assailed the loyalty of Catholics, and how little attention he has given to verify the statements on which his wanton attacks are founded.

The word "jus" is not, and should not be, confined to express civil rights exclusively. "Jus hominum", says Cicero, "situm est in generis humani societate". True, but there are two societies of men: civil society, or the state; ecclesiastical society, or the Church; and therefore, according to Mr. Gladstone's own theory as expressed in the quotation from Cicero, there are two classes of jura or rights—jura civilia, which pertain to the state or civil society, and jura ecclesiastica, which pertain to the Church or the ecclesiastical society. The proposition speaks of rights conferred on the Church by her Founder. What sort of rights are they? If they are ecclesiastical rights, Mr. Gladstone should not have translated them by the words civil rights; if they are civil rights, then the Church has civil rights conferred on her by her Founder; that is, she has CIVIL RIGHTS by DIVINE RIGHT !!!

Surely the Pope rightly condemned the proposition which granted to the State the power to limit the exercise of jura, which the Church holds by divine right.

The rights are called jura ecclesiæ. Who could translate jura ecclesiæ by the words "civil rights", whose mind was not warped by a factious spirit? The proposition asserts that the State has the right to define the limits of the rights of the Church. The Pope condemns it, and every Christian who sincerely believes in a Church founded by Christ, must assent to the condemnation. If the Church becomes the creature of the State, and permits the State to limit her divine rights and obstruct their exercise, like the Eastern Greek Church, the Russian Church, and the Church of England, she will soon lose her character of a Christian Church, and receive her doctrine, discipline, and government from the civil authority.

The next proposition to which Mr. Gladstone objects, is the 77th of the Syllabus, condemned in the Allocution, "*Acerbissimum*", September 30th, 1852:—"Huic laudabiliter in quibusdam Catholici nominis regionibus lege cantum est, ut omnibus illuc immigrantibus liceat publicum proprii cujuscumque cultus exercitium habere". I respectfully ask Mr. Gladstone, would it be laudable to provide by law, that a Mormon colony from Utah should have the free exercise of their religion in a Catholic nation or in any Christian nation? If he says no, it could not be laudable, then he agrees with the Papal condemnation; if he says yes, he stands alone amongst English Christian gentlemen. I appeal to the public opinion of the great English people, and I feel the most perfect confidence that, except on the questions of marriage and the use of force by the Church, the sound public opinion of England thoroughly assents to every condemnation in the Syllabus cited by Mr. Gladstone.

The next proposition cited in *Vaticanism* is the 25th of the Syllabus, condemned in "Ad Apostolicæ", Aug. 22, 1831:—"Præter potestatem Episcopa tui inhærentem aliâ est attributa temporalis potestas a civili imperio vel expresse vel tacite concessa revocanda propterea cum libuerit a civili potestate". Without the context of the work from which this proposition is taken, it is difficult to determine its precise meaning. It is quite clear, however, that in the context it may have had a sense which is evidently false, and may speak of a temporal power, or WHAT the writer called a TEMPORAL POWER of the episcopate, which no church could concede to the State the power of withdrawing at pleasure. The case of the Bishop of Durham, cited by Mr. Gladstone, or any similar case, could not have been contemplated in the proposition. An episcopal right, and a right conferred by the State on a particular bishop, are very different. The right of coinage was conferred on a bishop, but it was not a temporal right of the Episcopate.

The laws of the Church in Christian marriage are plain and simple, and though they may not be agreeable to Mr. Gladstone, the Church is not likely to change them at his bidding. Except one doubtful point settled by the present Holy Father, they are at the present day precisely as they were fixed by the Council of Trent. If Mr. Gladstone has been the champion of Catholic rights for thirty years of his life, it is difficult to see why the marriage laws excite his ire, for I am quite certain, if asked, he could not indicate the change introduced by the present Pope. The marriage laws of the Catholic Church are the basis of Christian society, and in proportion as they are disregarded, so are the beauties of the Christian family and the Christian home fast disappearing from amongst us, and the licentiousness and vice of the pagan world corrupting society to its very core. It is strange that Mr. Gladstone, with the records of the Divorce Court before him, could be so irate with the discipline of the Church on Christian marriage. He conveniently ignores facts of very recent occurrence. The history of the Yelverton-Longworth marriage case will not soon be forgotten, and painfully illustrates the state of the marriage laws of England at that period. True, these laws are now amended, and the invalidity of the marriage and the felony of the priest are no longer the consequences of celebrating a marriage between a Catholic and a Protestant in Ireland; but a gentleman who so lately lived in a glass house shows bad taste in throwing stones at his neighbours.

Mr. Gladstone states, and states truly, that the Church can, if she so pleases, publish the law of clandestinity, and subject to its force all Protestant marriages; but the question is not what the Church can do, but what the Church will do. All the declarations of the Church on the subject of clandestinity, and they are numerous, tend to exempt the marriages of non-Catholics from the obligation of the law.

Wherever a Protestant religious society existed before the promulgation of the law of clandestinity, the Church uniformly exempted its members from the obligations of the law, and even extended that exemption to the marriages of Protestants with Catholics. There is even a recent decision where this exemption is granted to persons who secede from the Catholic Church and join the Protestant communion. Nothing could more clearly indicate the mind of the Church than this decision. She certainly never will refuse to persons born in the Protestant Church an exemption which she grants to apostates, the class she most abhors. Judging, therefore, the future by the past, it is morally certain the Church will never extend the law of clandestinity to Protestant communities.

It is strange how peevish Mr. Gladstone seems to feel on this subject. Does he believe the law of clandestinity has any force to annul a Protestant marriage ? If not, why feel so apprehensive at the very remote possibility of its publication in England, especially as it cannot touch the contract of marriage in its civil effects ? If the law of clandestinity was published in England tomorrow, it is quite certain the privilege of the declaration of Benedict XIV. for Holland would be extended to the marriages of all non-Catholics.

Mr. Gladstone's last proposition is also the last proposition of the Syllabus. It is No. 80, and was condemned in the allocution "*Jandudum*", March 18th, 1861.

"Romanus Pontifex potest ac debet cum progressu cum liberalismo et cum recenti civilitate reconciliare et componere".

The Roman Pontiff—the ruler of the Church of God—in Mr. Gladstone's opinion, should be reconciled with modern progress and liberalism. Should he be reconciled with modern progress as represented by Strauss and Renan, which makes war on the Son of God? Mr. Gladstone's eloquent words at Liverpool prove that he is not himself reconciled with modern progress under this aspect; but perhaps the Holy Father should be reconciled with the modern progress of Tindall and Huxly, which is labouring to uproot the grounds of Christian faith; or perhaps he wishes to reconcile the Church with the liberalism of the French Communists or the modern civilization of the Italian Carbonari, which assails the very foundations of Christian society. If Mr. Gladstone would condescend to define the precise phase of modern progress which meets his approval, and with which he is so anxious to reconcile the Holy Father and the Christian Church, something might be done to appease the choleric ex-minister. Modern thought, modern progress, scientific discovery, social elevation, are very nice phrases; they are very much in vogue in this superficial age, and are splendid topics for the exercise of fluent rhetoric, in which Mr. Gladstone is so distinguished a proficient. But one would think a sincere believer in Christian revelation might have found some more useful theme for the exercise of his eloquence than an unprovoked attack on the only Church which can defend Christian truth and protect Christian society from the rising flood of unbelief. But Mr. Gladstone has another complaint against the Holy Father. I cite his words with regret :—" It appears to be claimed for Popes that they shall be superior over the laws of language ; but mankind protest against a system which palters in a double sense with its own solemn declarations, imposing them on the weak, glorying in them before those who are favourably prepossessed, and contracting their sense, *ad libitum*, even to the point of nullity, by arbitrary interpolations, to appease the scandalized understanding of Christian nations". Pius IX. used the language of his court, the language of his sublime office, language consecrated by his predecessors for eighteen centuries, language the most precise and definite in which human thought was ever cast ; and because the Holy Father does not abandon the language of the Church and of his exalted office, and adopt, I presume, the dialect of the press and the club-room, he is charged with sophistry, insincerity, and virtually with lying. This is a grave charge against the Supreme Pontiff of the Christian Church. No one mindful of his own dignity would have lightly made it; a whole treatise might be written in its refutation; but should Mr. Gladstone condescend to reply to these remarks, he owes it to his own character to justify this charge by evidence from the history of the Papacy. This is not the way in which honourable gentlemen usually treat each other. Pius IX. is a sovereign, the oldest and the most venerable in Europe, and yet Mr. Gladstone assails him in a style and manner in which he would not dare to address the lowest member of the House of Commons. I thought that refinement of feeling and scrupulous respect for the rights of others, for which gentlemen trained in the great universities of England are so eminently distinguished, would have saved Mr. Gladstone from this unseemly exhibition of petty spite.

The propositions of the Syllabus may be regarded in their individual or in their collective character—that is, we may regard each proposition in connection with the document in which it was first published, or we may consider them as collected from the several allocutions, formed into one document, and sent to the bishops of the Church. In their first publication, it is quite certain the propositions of the Syllabus were not dogmatic, for the allocutions from which they were extracted were not addressed to the Universal Church (which is an essential condition of a dogmatic bull), but to particular bishops.

It remains, then, to determine, did the Holy Father wish to give the propositions of the Syllabus any additional sanction in their collective form, as sent to all the bishops of the Church. It is now practically certain that he did not. Doctor Fesseler expresses a doubt of the dogmatic character of the Syllabus. This doubt was permitted by the Holy Father in his approval of the work, which practically settles the question. The form of the document, too, is not that of a dogmatic bull, and some of the matter, though most apt for the exercise of the Pope's supreme spiritual jurisdiction, seems to me not apt matter for the exercise of his defining power.

CHAPTER IV.

THE INFALLIBILITY OF THE POPE IS NOT A NEW DOCTRINE, BUT IS AS OLD AS THE PAPACY ITSELF.

"IT is an opinion held by great authorities, that no Pontiff before Leo X. attempted to set up the infallibility of Popes as a dogma" (*Vaticanism*, p. 54). Who these great authorities are Mr. Gladstone does not condescend to tell us. It is clear he has some distrust of their greatness, or he would not be so reticent of their names. One thing is quite certain,—they are not great authorities in theology or ecclesiastical history. It is a common delusion with great authorities of this class, that if a doctrine is newly defined it is therefore a new doctrine. Mr. Gladstone seems also of this opinion. The infallibility of the Church was never yet defined. Would he call it a new doctrine if it had formed the subject of a decree in the Vatican Council? If the precise phrase in which a doctrine is expressed in a subsequent definition is not found in the early ecclesiastical writers, it is no proof the doctrine was not believed in the early Church. We seek in vain in the Apostolic writings for the subtleties of phrase used in the Arian controversy. Will Mr. Gladstone infer that the divinity of the Son of God was not a doctrine of the Apostolic Church? The infallibility of the Pope was always the doctrine of the Church. Had it never been denied, it is probable it would never have been defined; and, at the period to which Mr. Gladstone refers, it was not the doctrine of infallibility, but its denial, which was a novelty in Catholic teaching. Gerson, who was one of the earliest patrons of the doctrine, admits that up to the time of the Council of Constance, all who denied the Infallibility of the Pope were condemned for heretical tendencies. I quote his words: "Before the celebration of this holy Council of Constance, this tradition or doctrine so swayed the minds of writers, that the teacher of opposite opinions was either suspected or condemned for heretical tendencies".

If the Infallibility was not of faith, those who condemned it would not be suspected of heretical tendencies, and yet Mr. Gladstone, to use his own phrase, says it was set up by Leo X. Major, another patron of Gallican opinions, says, "The opposite doctrine our University of Paris has held SINCE THE DAYS OF THE COUNCIL OF CONSTANCE". Here is the date of the birth of the Gallican error —"THE DAYS OF THE COUNCIL OF CONSTANCE"— and but for this error, we probably never would have had the definition of the Vatican Council. The heresy of Arius called forth the voice of the Church in the definition of Nicea. The error of the Gallicans called forth the definition of the Vatican, which but repeats and formulizes the faith of the Universal Church since the days of St. Peter. It could serve no good purpose to discuss the Scripture texts with Mr. Gladstone. The discussion would carry us beyond the limits of a pamphlet, and they have been so ably discussed in recent times that, to introduce the topic here, would appear a trite repetition. However, he may have some respect for the opinion of Origen, who is no mean witness of the faith of the early Church. He is commenting on the text, "Thou art Peter, and upon this rock I will build my

Church, and the gates of hell shall not prevail against it". Having asked himself to what the pronoun "it" refers, Origen says, "The phrase is ambiguous. In my opinion the true meaning is that the gates of hell shall prevail, neither against the rock upon which Christ built His Church, nor against the Church itself, for if the gates of hell should prevail against any one, it certainly would not be against the rock on which Christ built His Church, nor against the Church founded by Christ on the rock. The rock is inaccessible to the serpent, it is stronger than the gates of hell, which wage war against it; it is because of its very strength that they cannot prevail against it. The Church itself, Christ's building, who wisely built His house on Peter, has nothing to fear from the gates of hell. These have power only against him who finds himself separated from the rock and the Church". This is alarmingly like Infallibility. The following words of the same writer are still more so: "Consider what must be the power and authority of Peter, the living rock upon which the Church was built, and whose decisions have as much force and validity as oracles emanating from God Himself". Here is Origen, in the fourth century, teaching the Infallibility of the Pope as plainly as it was taught in the Vatican; and yet Mr. Gladstone coolly informs us it has only a chequered and intermittent life for six centuries.

I have before me, whilst I write, passages expressing the doctrine of Papal Infallibility, even more clearly than the texts from Origen, from the following Fathers and Councils. St. Iræneus, who had the Apostolic traditions from St. John, with but a single link intervening; St. Cyprian, who lived in the middle of the third century; St. Gregory Nazianzen; St. Ambrose; St. Jerome; St. Augustine; St. Cyril, who says, " As members of the mystical body of the Church, it is incumbent on us to follow one head, the Roman Pontiff, who holds in trust the deposit of apostolic faith. From him we must learn what we are bound to believe, think, and hold". St. Peter Chrysologus says, " Peter, who lives and governs his own see, returns to those who consult him the true faith". The Spanish Bishops, writing to Pope Hilary, say, We wait for an answer from that See whose decrees are never tainted with error. These clear testimonies of the Fathers are confirmed by letters of the following Pontiffs, in which the doctrine is expressed: Pope Damasus, Innocent I., Zozimus, Xystus III., Leo I., Simplicius, Gelasius, Hormisdas, Pelagius II., Gregory the Great, Leo II., Nicholas I.; and this testimony of Popes and Fathers is confirmed by the following Councils: Nicea, Constantinople first, Ephesus, Chalcedon, Constantinople second of, Constantinople third of, second of Nice; first, second, third, and fourth of Lateran; first of Lyons. Mr. Gladstone says there was no conciliary declaration. It is quite true there was no formal definition, but this was because there was no formal denial. The doctrine of papal infallibility was received and acted upon in the early Church, just like the doctrine of the infallibility of the Church, which was never defined because it was never denied; but if the Gallicans had lived in the second century, and not in the seventeenth, we would have had the definition of Papal Infallibility in Nicea, and not in the Vatican.

This is a question which could not be discussed incidentally in a popular pamphlet; but if Mr. Gladstone wishes to make the antiquity of the doctrine of Papal Infallibility the subject of a substantive controversy, he will find a host of champions anxious to enter the lists with him.

CHAPTER V.

THE SO-CALLED BREACHES WITH HISTORY ARE FROM MISCONCEPTIONS IN BREACH NO. I. MR. GLADSTONE CONFOUNDS DIVINE FAITH WITH CATHOLIC FAITH IN BREACH NO. II. HE IS NOT CORRECTLY INFORMED. OF THE VALUE OF THE DECREES OF THE COUNCILS OF CONSTANCE AND BASLE.

THE third chapter of *Vaticanism* is a proof of Mr. Gladstone's ignorance of the elementary principles of Catholic theology, and affords another illustration of the Horatian saw, " ne sutor". Few could believe that the modern champion of Gallicanism is ignorant of the distinction between DIVINE faith and CATHOLIC faith. Such were not the Gallicans of the olden time. They were versed in theological lore, and trained in scholastic subtlety, and went forth armed cap-a-pie to do battle for their opinions; but the last champion of their forlorn hope mounts the breach without cuirass or helmet, vulnerable by the arrows of the mere crossbowmen. Mr. Gladstone denies that the Infallibility of the Pope was an article of divine faith before the Vatican Council, and adduces, in proof of his denial, various bulls, briefs, and rescripts of Paul V., Urban VIII., Innocent X., and declarations of English Catholics and of Irish Bishops, which do not at all touch the question. They prove conclusively that Papal Infallibility was not an article of CATHOLIC faith; but they do not prove that the Infallibility was not of DIVINE faith. Every revealed truth in the whole deposit of revelation is of divine faith, but is not of Catholic faith until proposed by the Church for the belief of the faithful under pain of expulsion from her communion.

The Infallibility was not an article of Catholic faith until it was defined in the Vatican Council. It was an article of divine faith from the institution of the primacy; it became an article of Catholic faith after its definition. The great mission of the Church of God is to guard the deposit of revelation, and from century to century to take from it revealed truths, to formulize them, and propose them as articles of Catholic faith, to be believed by all who are in communion with her. In fulfilment of this great mission, Nicea defined the divinity of the Son of God, Constantinople defined the divinity of the Holy Ghost, Ephesus and Chalcedon added the doctrines of the two natures and the divine personality of Christ to the articles of Catholic faith. Thus, from the days of the Apostles, the Church of God, semper eadem, always acting on the same principles and guided by the same divine Spirit, has guarded the divine deposit of revelation, and added new articles to her creed, as, from time to time, the errors of the age required a more formal definition of doctrine to protect the integrity of Christian faith. The deposit of revelation cannot increase. It is now as it was on the death of St. John; but the Church has power from God to interpret that deposit infallibly, and to develope it by defining articles of CATHOLIC faith, which all her members are bound to believe under pain of expulsion from her communion.

Many bishops, before Nicea, did not believe the Divinity of the Son of God, and persisted in their error after the definition; a few bishops entered the Vatican Council, not believing the doctrine of Papal Infallibility, but, thank God, they are now amongst its sincerest believers and its most ardent supporters. The fact that a bishop or a number of bishops deny a doctrine, is no proof that the doctrine is not of divine faith, but proves conclusively that it is not of Catholic faith, that is, that it has not been defined by the Church as a doctrine to be believed by all who are in union with the chair of Peter. Hence Mr. Gladstone's mistake, and his first supposed breach with history. He finds that the English vicars apostolic and the Irish Catholic bishops published documents stating that the Infallibility of the Pope was not an article of Catholic faith, which was quite true; but they did not state, and could not state, that it was not of divine faith, believed and taught by the greater part of the Church of God. Nor did they state (and if they did it would be an act of great presumption) that the Infallibility of the Pope, though not then defined, might not one day receive the seal of the Church, and be added to the articles of the Catholic creed. It would be as if a few Arian bishops should promise a wicked Arian emperor, to appease his anger and mitigate his persecution, that the doctrine of the Divinity of the Son of God would never receive the formal definition of the Church.

The prevalence of the Gallican opinion in Ireland amongst the Bishops at that period, did not express the faith of the people. When Maynooth College was founded, many of its first professors were French priests who were driven from France by the Revolution. They taught this Gallican opinion to the clergymen educated there. In consequence of the persecution, many Irish priests were educated in French colleges, and brought back the erroneous doctrine which then tainted the French Church. But at any period of our history, if you told a pious Irish Catholic layman, that the Pope, the head of the Church of God, Christ's Vicar on earth, could teach heresy to the faithful when speaking as Pope to the Universal

Church, Paddy would regard the doctrine as rank heresy, and tell you it smelled strongly of Martin Luther.

His Eminence Cardinal Manning states, " that the civil allegiance of Catholics is as undivided as that of other Christians, and neither more nor less". Mr. Gladstone denies this proposition, but advances no argument in support of his denial. Will Mr. Gladstone admit that there is a moral obligation higher than the obligation of civil allegiance ? will he admit that conscience is the final interpreter of the line of moral duty, if these obligations clash ? This is the final test for Catholics: is it not the same for all Christians ? Are not all who acknowledge a higher Christian law, bound to refuse obedience to the State, if it demands as a civil duty what this Christian law condemns as intrinsically wrong? If Mr. Gladstone denies this, then he must hold that the martyrs, who, in obedience to the higher Christian law, resisted the state and died for the faith, were wrong, and that all who at any time in the world's history nobly suffered for duty, principle, honour, or faith, deserve, not our admiration but our censure. Does Mr. Gladstone wish a dead level of Cæsarism, where the State enters the sacred domain of conscience, and becomes the ultimate test of the obligations of moral duty? I cannot believe that the great and gifted chief of the Liberal party, the eloquent champion of civil and religious freedom, could become the advocate of the lowest form of the most degraded despotism.

The conscience of the Catholic, like the conscience of every other subject, must be for him the ultimate rule of right, and if the state demands what conscience cannot concede, all are alike bound to refuse obedience, whatever may be their form of religious belief. This is the limit and the sole limit to civil allegiance, and it is the same for all.

"The claim of the Roman Catholic Church against obedience to the civil power in certain cases is the same as that made by other religious communities". Mr. Gladstone denies this proposition: he should rather distinguish it. The principle of the claim is the same for all, but the practice of the Catholic Church is notably different. The Catholic Church has defined laws, defined principles of action, and a defined faith. She is a perfect society, with her rights, legislative, judicial, and coercive, and can never, therefore, be absorbed by the state like the other so-called Christian Churches. She cannot take her faith from the state like Mr. Gladstone's Church, nor her discipline, nor her laws of moral duty, but she must preach obedience to the civil law and loyalty to the sovereign, unless the civil law demands what Christian duty forbids : then her children must refuse obedience, and suffer for justice sake. The Catholic Church can never become the mere creature of the state. She has no Indian-rubber principles, which can be dragged to any length to meet requirements and suit circumstances. Her motto is an inflexible "non possumus". She is a great bulwark to resist the oppressive encroachments of ambitious sovereigns on human liberty, and to protect the sacred rights of conscience. This has been in every age a secondary mission of the Church of God, and admits of the clearest proof from history. The Reformers would hand over the human conscience to the tender keeping of temporal rulers, but the Church of God interposed her inexorable veto against this iniquitous bargain. They would barter human liberty for a licence to preach their reformed faith, which is simply Catholicity stript of everything difficult to believe and hard to practise.

The Gallican objections from the Councils of Constance and Basle are new to Mr. Gladstone and to many of his readers; to students of ecclesiastical history and theology they are old acquaintances, familiar as household words. A brief history of the council is the simplest refutation of the objection.

At the suggestion of Sigismund, afterwards emperor, John XXIII. called a council at Constance, which assembled in 1414, and held its first session on the 16th of November.

In the fourth session, held on the 30th of March, was passed the decree on which Mr. Gladstone rests his thesis, that the Council is superior to the Pope. The following is the form of the decree according to Cardinal Turrecremata, who was present in the council: "Hæc sancta synodus Constantiensis generale concilium faciens pro extirpatione presentis schismatis et unione ac reformatione Ecclesiæ in capite et in membris fienda declarat quod ipsa in spiritu sancto congregata Generale Concilium faciens et Ecclesiam Catholicam militantem representans potestatem a Christo habet immediate cui quilibet cujuscunque status vel dignitatis etsi papalis existat obedire tenetur in his quæ pertinent ad fidem et extirpationem dicti schismatis". When this Council of Constance met, there were three claimants of the Papacy—John XXIII., Angelus Corarius Gregory XII., and Peter de Luna Benedict XIII. There was, therefore, no certain Pope, but there was a schism in the Church which the Council was assembled to heal.

The decree does not state the ordinary relation of Papal to Conciliar authority, but states that pro EXTIRPATIONE SCHISMATIS, the Pope is bound to obey the Council. This is clear from the words of the decree, which I have quoted; but, to remove all doubt, we have the testimony of Cardinal Turrecremata, who was present in the Council, stating that the words *pro extirpatione schismatis*, were specially introduced by the Council to restrict the force of this decree to the time of schism.

This was not the decree of a general council. It was passed in the fourth session, when there were none present but the followers of John, who could not be said to form a general council representing the Universal Church. The followers of Gregory XII. and Benedict XIII. were not summoned, and reclaimed against the Council as invalidly convoked. The council was not, therefore, as we say technically, œcumenical in convocation. Neither was the council œcumenical in celebration, for the bishops voted by nations, and not individually, as was the universal custom in the Church, and votes of priests and even of laymen were received. Hence the decree was not passed CONCILIARITER, and finally it was never confirmed by Martin V., 1st, because the decree of the fourth and fifth sessions was not reënacted, but was virtually cancelled by the following decree, which was passed when the followers of Gregory XII. and Benedict XIII. joined the assembly, and it became œcumenical. " Sacrosancta synodus Constantiensis statuit et decrevit quod futurus Romanus Pontifex per dei gratiam de proximo assumendus cum hoc sacro concilio vel deputandus per singulas nationes, debeat reformare Ecclesiam", etc. The function of reforming the Church, which, in the canon of the fourth session, was reserved to the Council, is, in this canon, confided to the future Pope. 2nd, Martin condemned a proposition of Huss, which denied to St. Peter supreme authority over the whole Church. Martin, as his successor, possessed the same authority as St. Peter. 3rd, The Council humbly asks from Pope Martin confirmation of its decrees. A superior authority does not ask an inferior to confirm its acts. 4th, Pope Martin confirmed only the acts of the Council which were passed CONCILIARITER " sic conciliareter facta approbat et ratificat et NON ALITER NEC ALIOMODO".—Form of Confirmation of Martin V. I have shown that the decree of the fourth session was not passed CONCILIARITER. It was not, therefore, confirmed by Pope Martin.

The doctrine of the fourth session of the Council of Constance was condemned in the following words found in the eleventh session of the fifth Council of Lateran: " Solum Romanum Pontificem pro tempore existentem auctoritatem super omnia concilia habere ex S. Scripturæ testimonio dictis sanctorum patrum ac aliorum Romanorum Pontificum prædecessorum nostrorum sacrorumque canonum decretis etiam propria conciliorum confessione constet".

In page 60 of *Vaticanism* Mr. Gladstone says : " We arrive then at the following dilemma :— Either that decree had full validity by the confirmation of the Pope, or Martin the Fifth was not a Pope, the Cardinals made or confirmed by him were not Cardinals, and could not elect validly his successor, Eugenius IV. ; so that the papal succession has failed since an early date in the fifteenth century, or more than four hundred and fifty years ago".

Mr. Gladstone is too acute to be deceived by this sophistry, but he is quite certain it is sufficiently plausible to deceive the great majority of his readers. The decree of Constance has no validity by the confirmation of the Pope, and yet Martin the Fifth was true and legitimate Pope.

The fallacy Mr. Gladstone so adroitly introduces supposes that the validity of Pope Martin's election depended on the validity of the decree. This is evidently untrue, and even whilst he wrote it there is one little telltale word which shows that Mr. Gladstone himself saw the fallacy. If the Council of Constance had not the power to set aside the several claimants to the Papacy, and to elect a successor, it is quite clear no decree of the Council could confer this power, for no assembly can give to itself by a decree a power which it does not already possess. A decree in such case is a mere form of words, declaratory of the power of the Council, but is not an instrument conferring that power; and whether the declaratory decree was valid or invalid, the exercise of the power which the Council already possessed is equally effective.

Mr. Gladstone knew this right well when framing his ingenious " argumentum cornutum "; his mind is too keen not to see the fallacy of supposing that a Council could confer on itself, by a mere form of words, a power which it did not already possess.

Independently of the decree, the Council of Constance, when it became Œcumenical, had the power to set aside the three pretenders to the Papacy, and to elect a legitimate Pope. In case of schism, when there are several aspirants to the papal chair, a General Council has power immediately from God to set aside the claimants, and to elect a successor to the See of Peter.

It is clear the decree of Constance could derive no force from Pope Martin's confirmation; for if it was not valid independently of his confirmation, Martin V. was not a legitimate Pope, for the decree deposing the rival claimants must have taken effect before he could be lawfully elected.

Mr. Gladstone need not be at all alarmed about the papal succession. Independently of all previous proceedings, the acceptance of Martin V. by the Universal Church as lawful Pope proves that his election was canonical and legitimate; for the recognition of the true Pope is a dogmatic fact in which the Universal Church cannot err. But, says Mr. Gladstone, the decree of Constance was confirmed by Basle, which was also a General Council. We cannot be expected to repeat here the dreary history of the Council of Basle. A few facts will dispose of Mr. Gladstone's objection.

In the year 1423, Martin V., according to a promise given at Constance, convoked a Council at Pavia; it was transferred to Sienna, and after the first session was dissolved. At the urgent request of the Bishops, Martin again convoked the Council at Basle. This convocation was confirmed by his successor Eugenius IV., and the Council met at Basle, in the church of St. Leonard, on the 7th of December, 1431, and held its first session on the 14th. After the first session, Pope Eugenius dissolved the Council of Basle, and after eighteen months appointed it to meet at Bologna, to consider the important question of union with the Greek Church. The Council refused to obey the Pope, proceeded to hold its second session on the 15th of March, 1432, and confirmed the famous decree of Constance, which places the authority of the Council above the Pope. At this session there were just fourteen prelates, eight bishops and six abbots. This imposing assembly of eight bishops and six abbots, after they had been dissolved by Pope Eugenius, declared themselves an authority superior to the Roman Pontiff; and this is the confirmation of the decree of Constance by eight bishops and six abbots, on which Mr. Gladstone rests so confidently as the decree of a general council. Between the second session and the seventeenth session this decree of Constance was reënacted fifteen times at Basle, but in the seventeenth session, on the 29th of July, 1433, peace was restored between the Council and Eugenius IV., and all the decrees against the authority of the Pope were annulled. On the 14th of September, 1437, Pope Eugenius published a bull transferring the council to Ferrara. After this all the cardinals, except D'Allemand of Arles, left the Council of Basle and joined the Pope at Ferrara, so that there remained at Basle only twenty-five bishops and seventeen abbots, whilst there were one hundred and sixty bishops at Ferrara, under the presidency of the Pope.

The discussion of the famous decree of Constance was again raised at Basle in the thirty-second session, in which only three bishops supported the Cardinal of Arles. But in the thirty-third session, all the bishops, except seven or eight, remained away, fearing the violence of the four hundred followers of Cardinal D'Allemand, and the decree of Constance was confirmed by one cardinal, seven or eight bishops, thirteen abbots, and four hundred priests; and this Mr. Gladstone calls the confirmation of a general council. And remember this decree was passed at Basle when Pope Eugenius was presiding over a General Council of one hundred and sixty bishops, which subsequently, when sitting at Florence, annulled the declaration of the schismatical conventicle of Basle in a formal decree, which received the undoubted confirmation of the Pope. Æneas Sylvius also, who was at the Council of Basle in the retinue of Cardinal Capranica, and supported the opponents of Pope Eugenius and the adherents of this doctrine, subsequently, when raised to the papal chair, abjured the doctrine in a formal bull.

Did Nicholas the Fifth confirm the acts of the Council of Basle?

If Nicholas the Fifth confirmed all the acts of the Council of Basle, and if they were valid, he would not be himself lawful Pope; for one of the acts in the thirty-fourth session was to depose

Pope Eugenius, and in the thirty-ninth session to elect Amadeus, Duke of Savoy, to the Papacy, under the title of Felix V.

Felix was still living, so that if the acts of the Council were valid, Felix V. was the true Pope, and Nicholas V. was an usurper and an anti-Pope.

What portion of the acts of the Council of Basle did Nicholas V. confirm?

During the protracted contest between the Pope and the Council, much confusion arose in the regulation of benefices, immunities, exemptions, dispensations, privileges, and other ecclesiastical concessions.

To disturb these concessions, even though granted invalidly by the Council, would cause new disturbances in the Church, and raise up a host of enemies against Pope Nicholas. He therefore wisely confirmed the acts of the Council in these matters of discipline, but withheld his confirmation from its acts as far as they violated the rights of the Holy See. This appears from the fact, that Pope Nicholas only ratified the confirmation of Pope Eugenius, in which this reservation is found in express terms.

CHAPTER VI.

THE POPE IS NOT "PRIMUS INTER PARES", BUT HAS ALWAYS EXERCISED SUPREME JURISDICTION IN THE WHOLE CHURCH.

THERE is, perhaps, no other question in ecclesiastical history, of which the evidence is so clear and so abundant, as of the supreme authority of the Bishop of Rome over the Universal Church. The appeals, judgments, depositions, and the conduct of Popes in general councils, are so numerous, and afford evidence so conclusive of the supreme authority of the Bishop of Rome, that one cannot guess why Mr. Gladstone represents him as only "primus inter pares". These facts are found in every manual of Church history, and are familiar to every student.

If the Pope is only "primus inter pares", why did the fifth General Council, convoked by Justinian, seek confirmation from the Roman Pontiff, and derive its authority solely from that confirmation? When the Pope condemned the Pelagians, if he spoke merely as an equal, why did St. Augustine say, "Roma locuta est, causa finita est"? The legates of Pope Leo condemned Dioscorus because he presumed to hold a general council without the authority of the Apostolic See; and Pelagius

II. asserts that this was the exclusive prerogative of Rome. As Primate of the whole Church the Pope always presided at General Councils. Thus Vitus and Vincentius, though only priests, presided at Nicea; St. Cyril presided at Ephesus, as the delegate of Pope Celestine; St. Leo deputed Paschasius and Lucentius to preside at Chalcedon; and the bishops, writing to St. Leo, say, " that by his delegates he had presided over them as the HEAD over MEMBERS". The epistles of the Roman Pontiffs, edited by Coustang, afford authentic evidence of the primacy to the pontificate of Pope Siricius, who, in one of his letters, tells us that Pope Liberius addressed a decree to the WHOLE Church, prohibiting the rebaptizing of persons who had been baptized by Arians. Innocent I. sent imperative instructions to Alexander, Patriarch of Antioch, on the ordination of bishops. The Bishops of Africa ask Pope Anastatius to dispense the canons of the Synod of Capua in favour of the Donatists.

The patriarchal system prevailed in the East, as Mr. Gladstone informs us, but it was in complete subjection to the See of Rome. The Roman Pontiff exercised supreme jurisdiction over the patriarchs, and, through them, over the whole Eastern Church.

The first act of the newly-elected patriarch was

to seek confirmation from the Pope, which was granted in "the Letters of Communion". Thus Theodosius I. asks confirmation of the election of Nectarius, Patriarch of Constantinople, St. John Chrysostom sent Acacius to ask the Pope to confirm his appointment. In like manner, Pope Leo confirms Anatolius of Constantinople, and Maximus of Antioch. Pope Simplicius confirmed John Talaia as Patriarch of Alexandria, but subsequently cancelled the appointment. The Pope was also the supreme judge over the patriarchs, and a sentence against a patriarch was invalid if not confirmed by the Pope. Thus Pope Julius annulled the sentence against St. Athanasius, though pronounced by a Council of Oriental bishops. Innocent I. cancelled the sentence against St. John Chrysostom. Juvenal of Jerusalem and John of Antioch claim their right to be judged only by the Bishop of Rome. Timothy of Alexandria, Peter of Antioch, Paul of Ephesus, and Acacius of Constantinople, were all deposed by Popes; and Gelasius, replying to Euphamius, asserts that the judgment of bishops was always the right of the Holy See.

If this is the conduct of a "primus inter pares", I should like to hear Mr. Gladstone's description of the action of a superior over inferiors. The Pope was the judge of all, and was to be judged by none. Thus when Theoderic called the bishops together, to pass judgment on Pope Symmachus, the bishops denied their competency, and said the Pope could not be placed in judgment before his own subjects. Bishops and Patriarchs from every part of the Universal Church appealed to the judgment of the Roman Pontiff, and these appeals were formally recognized and regulated in the Council of Sardica.

Let us now examine the acts of the eighth General Council, on which Mr. Gladstone rests his statement. Fortunately he could not have chosen an incident in the whole range of ecclesiastical history which more strikingly illustrates the recognition and the exercise of the supreme jurisdiction of the Roman Pontiff.

Ignatius, the lawful patriarch, was driven from Constantinople by the Emperor Bardas, Photius was obtruded into the see, and consecrated by Asbestas, the deposed bishop of Syracuse. The first act of the new patriarch was to send ambassadors to Pope Nicholas to ask CONFIRMATION of his appointment. Pope Nicholas writes, complaining that Ignatius had been deposed without the authority of the See of Rome. He required that the case of Ignatius should be examined in a synod in which his legates, Zacharias and Rodvald, should preside, and reserved the final judgment to himself. When Nicholas received the acts of the synod, in which **Ignatius** was deposed, he degraded his two legates, and declared that he did not consent to the deposition of Ignatius or the elevation of Photius, and sent this declaration to all the patriarchs, and to Photius and the emperor. In 863 he called a synod, and formally deposed Photius, and threatened excommunication if he held possession of the see of Constantinople, or obstructed Ignatius, the legitimate patriarch. He also deposed all the bishops consecrated by Photius, and declared null all the proceedings against Ignatius. The acts of this Council were formally confirmed in the eighth General Council, in the 2nd canon, as Mr. Gladstone admits, and yet he coolly informs us that this Council represents the Pope in his relations with the patriarchs as a " primus inter pares".

Photius asked confirmation of Pope Nicholas. Do dignitaries of equal rank ask confirmation of each other? The Pope annulled the proceedings of Photius against Ignatius. Has one bishop the power to annul the proceedings of another bishop of equal jurisdiction? The Pope deposed Photius. Is this the act of an equal? The Pope annulled the sentence against Ignatius, and restored him to his see. If Photius, Ignatius, and Nicholas were of equal authority, as Mr. Gladstone informs us, would not this conduct of Pope Nicholas be justly regarded as an outrageous usurpation?

All these acts of Pope Nicholas are evidently the exercise of supreme authority, and all these acts were formally confirmed by the eighth General Council, as the legitimate exercise of the supreme authority of the Roman See. The FORMAL CONFIRMATION of the jurisdiction expressed in these acts of Pope Nicholas, is a VIRTUAL RECOGNITION, as His Eminence Cardinal Manning expresses it, of the following canon, passed in a previous council held at Rome in the same year:—" Si quis dogmata mandata interdicta sanctiones, vel decreta pro catholica fide, pro ecclesiastica disciplina, pro correctione fidelium pro emendatione sceleratorum vel interdictione imminentium, vel futuorum malorum a sedis apostolicæ præside salubriter, promulgata contempserit anathema sit".—*Harduin's Councils*, vol. 5, year 863, page 574, Paris edition.

The legates of Pope Adrian, in the eighth General Council, were Donatus and Stephen, bishops, and Marinus, a deacon. In the fifth session, when Photius is introduced, and refuses to answer, the papal legates thus address him:—
" Ecce homo qui obturavit aures suas sicut aspydis surdæ et non audit vocem quam ei sancta synodus objicit sed vult per silentium hanc effugere con-

demnationem quam SANCTA ROMANA Ecclesia promulgavit adversus eum. Nos ergo", continue the legates, "non novum aliquod vel recens judicium judicavimus aut introducemus sed vetus ex multo tempore judicatum a beatissimo Papa Nicolao; firmatum autem a sanctissimo Papa Adriano". The bishops reply : "Recipimus hæc omnia valde quippe sunt discreta et congrua ecclesiasticis regulis". It appears, therefore, that the Bishops and Patriarchs of the eighth General Council received and approved, as in accordance with ecclesiastical discipline, the sentence of deposition pronounced by Pope Nicholas, and confirmed by Pope Adrian, against the Patriarch Photius. Therefore this was not an individual act of an individual Pope, as Mr. Gladstone would wish us to believe, but was, as the Bishops express it, an act " congrua ecclesiasticis regulis".

The following is the first subscription to the Council : " Ego Donatus gratia Dei Episcopus sanctæ Ostiensis Ecclesiæ locum obtinens Domini mei Hadriani summi Pontificis et UNIVERSALIS Papæ omnia quæ superius leguntur huic sanctæ et universali synodo præsidens usque ad voluntatem ejusdem eximii præsuli promulgavi et manu propia subscripsi". In the next place Stephen, and in the third place Marinus, the other two legates, and after them, Ignatius the Patriarch, sign the acts of the Council. The recognition of the supreme authority of the Roman Pontiff in the eighth General Council is beyond the possibility of cavil. The canons which Mr. Gladstone quotes make no reference to the relations of the Patriarchs to the Roman Pontiff. They but regulate the internal action of the Patriarchs in their respective Patriarchates.

In the East the civil power continued to encroach on the jurisdiction of the Patriarchs, and to obstruct their free action in the government of the Church. The seventeenth and twenty-first canons seek to strengthen the Patriarchs against the aggression of the state, by granting them a more complete power over their suffragans and metropolitans in synodical action, similar to the jurisdiction exercised by the Pope as PATRIARCH of the West. The twenty-sixth regulates the order of appeals.

CHAPTER VII.

OBEDIENCE TO THE POPE IS NOT CHANGED BY THE DECREES OF THE VATICAN COUNCIL.

BEFORE the definition of the Vatican Council bishops were supposed to have the abstract right to reclaim against a Papal decree, if they believed it contrary to faith or morals, a right, be it remembered, which the bishops never exercised, as since the Council we know they could not. Since the Vatican Council this abstract right does not exist, and Papal definitions are now declared infallible, independently of the tacit consent of the Church. This is the sole difference in the conditions of obedience to the Pope, before and after the Council of the Vatican. I should be glad to see how this abstract and purely speculative difference can fairly be made the basis of the vast superstructure of practical consequences for which Mr. Gladstone makes it responsible. The difference exists only in matters of faith and morals: in matters of jurisdiction there is no difference whatever in the conditions of obedience to the Pope before and since the publication of the Vatican Decrees. The Pope possessed at all times, and exercised at all times, the jurisdiction which the Vatican Council defined.

At page 68 Mr. Gladstone says: " Had the Decrees of 1870 been in force in the 16th and 17th centuries, Roman Catholic peers could not have done what until the reign of Charles II. they did—could not have made their way to the House of Lords by taking the oath of allegiance despite the Pope's commands". The Decrees of the Vatican could have no possible influence in this case. The

Pope's commands were not an exercise of his defining power, but of his supreme spiritual jurisdiction. He possessed and exercised the same spiritual jurisdiction in the 16th and 17th centuries which the Vatican Council defined, and peers had the same power in 1870 to disregard the Pope's commands as they had at any previous period.

This fact is so clear that it is difficult to understand how it could be unknown to Mr. Gladstone, and if he was aware of it, it is still more strange how he could have put forth such distorted views of Catholic doctrine as a justification of his charge of disloyalty against the Catholics of the Empire.

The Pope never bid the Catholics of England, or of any other nation, believe in the defining power as an article of faith. The part of the bull *Unam sanctum*, which refers to the deposing power, is not an ex cathedra declaration. That the Pope possessed and exercised such a power is matter of history; by what right he possessed and exercised it, it is not necessary to discuss, as it has no bearing on the present controversy. The question of the deposing power, and all similar acts which are the exercise of the Pope's jurisdiction, and not of his defining power, are in precisely the same condition as they were before the Vatican Council met, and afford no justification for the strange attitude Mr. Gladstone assumed in his *Expostulation* and *Vaticanism*. The very bulls he cites of Paul III., Pius V., etc., are the clearest proof that, at that time at least, the Popes exercised the supreme jurisdiction which the Vatican Council defined.

CHAPTER VIII.

IN HIS CHARGE AGAINST THE CHURCH OF THE USE OF FORCE, MR. GLADSTONE HAS NOT PROVED THAT THE WORD "VIS" IN THE CONDEMNED PROPOSITION MEANS MORE THAN THE ECCLESIASTICAL PUNISHMENT OF THE EXTERNAL COURT.

The Church of God has a twofold court, and jurisdiction in both by divine right. The punishments in the external court are coercive, and could be easily misunderstood by persons reading of their exercise. Aetius, Huss, Luther, Calvin, Grotius, and a host of more modern writers, denied that the Church had coercive jurisdiction, and confined her functions exclusively to the internal court, where admonition, exhortation, and council, were her sole weapons of correction. This error was first condemned by John XXII. in the brief *Licet juxta doctrinam*. Laborde granted the Church an external court, but subjected its exercise to the civil state. Benedict XIV. condemned this error in the bull *Ad Assiduas*, March 4th, 1755. It was also condemned by Pius VI. in *Auctorem fide;* and, finally, in the proposition of the Syllabus, on which Mr. Gladstone rests his present charge. The proposition is the 24th, and was condemned in *Ad Apostolicæ*, Aug. 22nd, 1851: " Ecclesia vis inferendæ potestatem non habet". What is the precise nature of the " vis" in the above proposition is not clearly determined: hence Mr. Gladstone's argument is not conclusive. If we refer to similar propositions condemned by Pius VI., they incline us to believe that the word " vis" in the above proposition means nothing more than the exercise of a coercive force by censures, excommunications, and similar ecclesiastical penalties inflicted by the Church in her external forum.

The following is the proposition condemned by Pius VI. : " Abusum fore auctoritatis Ecclesiæ transferendo illam ultra limites doctrinæ ac morum et eam extendendo ad res exteriores et per vim exegendo id quod pendet a persuasione et corde tum etiam multo minus ad eam pertinere exigere per vim exteriorem subjectionem suis decretis". In the condemnation of this proposition we find the following words : " Quatenus intendat Ecclesiam non habere collatam sibi a Deo potestatem non solum dirigendi per concilia et suasiones sed etiam jubendi per leges ac devios contumacesque exteriore judicio ac salubribus pœnis coercendi atque cogendi". The "vis" referred to in this proposition is clearly the vis of the external court, as opposed to mere exhortation and council. The exercise of this vis is a power given to the Church by God of passing laws for the direction of her subjects, and of enforcing their observance on the contumacious by citing them to her court, and restraining them, if necessary, by salutary punishments which that court inflicts.

In the absence of proof to the contrary, is it not fair to infer that the word " *vis*" in the proposition of the Syllabus has the same meaning as in the Auctorem fidei, and in the condemnations of John XXII. and Benedict XIV. ? There was no new doctrine put forth in the Syllabus on the use of force by the Church; hence Mr. Gladstone, who was for years the champion of the civil rights of Catholics, is not justified in his present policy.

The coercive power vindicated to the Church by Pius IX. is precisely the same as that vindicated by John XXII., Benedict XIV., and Pius VI. Their constitutions condemned the Erastian error which endeavoured to strip the Church of the legislative, judicial, and coercive power given to her by Christ, and to make her a creature of the state, dependent on the civil power for the exercise of her jurisdiction.

The vis intended in all the decrees is indicated by St. Paul in the Second Epistle to the Corinthians, x. 8 : " For if I should boast somewhat more of our power which the Lord hath given us for edification and not for your destruction". And again in the thirteenth chapter, tenth verse : "Therefore I write these things, being absent, that being present I may not deal more severely according to the power which the Lord hath given me to edification and not to destruction". And again, in the first Epistle to the Corinthians, chap. v., verses 4, 5 : " In the name of our Lord Jesus Christ you being gathered together, and my spirit with the power of our Lord Jesus Christ, to deliver such a one to Satan for the destruction of the flesh, that the spirit may be saved in the day of our Lord Jesus Christ". This is clearly a judicial and coercive act. Again, in the second Epistle to the Thessalonians, chap. iii., verses 14, 15 : " And if any man obey not our word by this epistle, note that man, and do not keep company with him, that he may be ashamed". And again, Titus, chap. iii., verse 10 : " A man that is a heretic after the first and second admonition avoid". The judicial and coercive force indicated in these texts is the same as that vindicated to the

Church by John XXII., Benedict XIV., Pius VI., and Pius IX. What that force may be, how far it may extend, and what precise forms of punishments it may include, are questions beside the present controversy. It is clear, however, it is no new doctrine put forth for the first time by the Syllabus, but its exercise by the Church is as old as the days of St. Paul.

CHAPTER IX.

THE VATICAN DECREES INTRODUCED NO FLAWS INTO THE CIVIL ALLEGIANCE OF CATHOLICS.

ONE would think Mr. Gladstone might have prudently avoided this topic. If the Church of Rome be a Christian Church at all, it is clear she has from God the right and the duty to expound to her subjects the laws of Christian faith and moral duty, to explain their meaning, their significance, their binding force, and to define when circumstances may change or modify the nature and extent of their obligations. This, I presume, Mr. Gladstone will admit, is the right and the duty of every Church. The whole question, then, narrows itself to this one point. In this exposition of doctrine and duty to her subjects, is the Church to be subject to, and to be guided by, the state? If Mr. Gladstone says yes, the Church must be subject to the state in her expositions of doctrine, discipline, and morals. The Roman Catholic Church, before and after the Vatican Council, and for all time since her foundation by Christ, is not the Church after his ideal standard. If Mr Gladstone says no, the Church of God should not be subject to the state in her expositions of Christian faith, and of the obligations of moral duty. She is herself the judge and exponent commissioned by Christ, and, in this department, is independent of, and superior to, the state. If this is Mr. Gladstone's opinion, he should find no fault with the Vatican decrees, but should quickly come forth from the Church, of which he is so distinguished a member. Mr. Russell Gurney's bill, when it becomes law, will give a little light to Mr. Gladstone, of which he seems sadly in need.

Does the 37th article, which grants to the king all power, civil and ecclesiastical, express the doctrine of the Apostolic Church? Few good men in England think so: many endeavour to explain it away, many evade its force, and not a few were driven by it from what they regarded as a mere human institution resting on civil law, to seek refuge in the Church of God, commissioned by Christ to teach independently of civil authority.

Does Mr. Gladstone expect Catholics to adopt Filmer's theory of divine right, or the teaching of Elizabeth's bishops, that no form of Church government is divinely ordained, that the state may lawfully abolish or establish episcopacy, and that the authority of a bishop, as Macaulay says, is in the same category as the authority of the sheriff and the coroner. What is this but Turkish despotism, the very absolutism which Mr. Gladstone so eloquently denounces? What says the early Christian Church on this theory of Mr. Gladstone's, which would elevate the human above the divine law, and constitute the Church the slave of the State? If Mr. Gladstone happened to live in a Mohammedan state, and that a law was passed imposing the obligation of bigamy on all the subjects of the realm, would he obey? If he declines to take unto himself a second helpmate in the Lord, there is clearly a flaw in his allegiance. What is the history of the early Church during the famous ten persecutions but the history of a divided allegiance, perfectly analogous to the divided allegiance of Catholics, of which Mr. Gladstone complains? We are prepared to give to Cæsar what belongs to Cæsar, and to obey his laws when they do not derogate from the law of God, and invade the sacred domain of conscience ; but when State laws are unjust, when they ask what belongs not to Cæsar but to God, we answer, with St. Peter and with the martyrs, and with all the glorious host who have suffered in defence of Christian liberty, " We must obey God rather than man "; or we reply, in the brief but eloquent words of the glorious prisoner of the Vatican, " Non possumus".

" Desine quæso te et mihi obtempera Constanti hæc enim et me decet scribere et te non vilipendere. Ne te rebus misceas ecclesiastics neu nobis his de rebus præcepta mandes sed a nobis potius hæc ediscas". This sentiment of a bishop of the early Church is not much in accordance with Gladstonianism, and if uttered by Pius IX., would have formed the text of a page in *Vaticanism*. " Nam vos quoque imperio meo ac throno lex Christi subjicit". Clearly, St. Gregory was not a Gladstonian—" Alii sunt termini regni alii sacerdotii verum hoc illo majus est". This sentiment of St. John Chrysostom is a striking contrast to Mr. Gladstone's principle of ideal allegiance. It is useless to cite passages to prove what no Christian can deny, and what the whole history of God's Church testifies — the right of the Church to teach her subjects the doctrines of Christian faith and the obligations of moral duty, independently of the authority of the State. This right extends to the duty of civil allegiance, as to all other duties involved in the complex circle of daily life. This right the Church claims to-day, this right she claimed in every age from the days of the Apostles; there is no other claim so clearly written in her history, so constantly inscribed on her banner. It is the great charter of Christian liberty, which has constituted her the enemy of tyrants and the guardian of freedom in every age of her history.

Mr. Gladstone is a member of the Church of England. How far does he recognize her right to interpret for him the obligations of moral duty? Up to that limit, whatever it may be, his allegiance is divided. The same is true for every one who acknowledges any authority in the Church or *quasi* Church to which he belongs: the same is true for Catholics, with this notable difference, that they are more docile to the guidance of their Church than the members of the other religious communities. Will Mr. Gladstone contend that Catholics must take his practice as the measure of the extent to which they should receive the direction of their Church as the exponent of their conscientious duty? If not, he can find no fault with their allegiance. They obey the civil law until the higher law of conscience interposes. So does Mr. Gladstone, so do all the other subjects of her majesty. The principle for all is strictly the same; the application of the principle varies according to the extent to which members of the several Churches receive the direction of their Church as the interpreter of that higher law.

CHAPTER X.

ON THE INTRINSIC NATURE OF PAPAL INFALLIBILITY MR. GLADSTONE IS NOT CORRECTLY INFORMED.

THE chapter on the intrinsic nature of Papal Infallibility is the most shadowy in *Vaticanism*, and suggests the suspicion that here, at least, the gifted author is getting somewhat out of his depth. It is a species of nebulous cloud floating indistinctly before the mind of the writer, to which he has not yet given shape and form. Like the Brocken spectre, it looks formidable at a distance, but as you approach, it dwindles to vacuity, and vanishes, and if you attempt to seize it, sylph-like, it evades your grasp. Catholics quite agree with Bishop Thirlwall on the vast importance of the definition, but they estimate its consequences very differently. He regards it as the ruin, we as the crowning triumph, of the Christian Church. The miseries of Basle and Constance can never be repeated, nor the hideous hydra of schism again afflict the

Church of God, and disturb the faith of her children. The Christian religion is not in the heart of the Pope, nor suspended on his will, but God has constituted the Pope the supreme ruler of the Christian Church, and promised him divine aid to discharge faithfully the duties of his sublime office. The Christian religion is in the heart of the Pope neither more nor less than it was since the days of St. Peter. At all times a Papal decree *ex cathedra* became an article of faith by the tacit consent of the Church—a consent which was never withheld. Since the Vatican Council, this consent is not required. This is the sole change introduced by the Council—a change which cannot possibly affect Christian faith in any of the relations of daily life.

Mr. Gladstone has the good taste to compare a dogmatic decree emanating from the Pope with an act of Parliament emanating from the Legislature. He is clearly fond of a *constitutional* article of faith, resting on a majority of the House of Commons for its validity. In this he is consistent, for though in words he may deny (as a member of the Church of England), in fact he must receive, the authority of Parliament as superior to the authority of his Church in discipline, in government, and in doctrine also, at least when Mr. Russell Gurney's bill becomes law. If Papal Infallibility depended upon human aid for its incrrancy, Mr. Gladstone's reasoning is at least plausible; but as Catholics hold and believe that the dogmatic decrees of the Roman Pontiff are preserved from error, not by the devices of men, but by the aid of heaven, his argument is worse than silly. Mere human means could not give infallibility to Church or Pope, but if God chooses to raise up an infallible interpreter of His law, He can secure inerrancy to an individual as easily as to the whole Church. Is Papal Infallibility more incredible than the gift of prophecy conferred on individuals in the old law? is it more wonderful than the power given to Josue or Moyses, or than the inspiration given to the evangelists, who were individually infallible, and spoke the word of God Himself? Mr. Gladstone's view of Papal Infallibility is grossly rationalistic. He rejects it because it is repugnant to his notions that God should constitute an individual the infallible exponent of revealed truth, and seems to think such a power could rest only with a body restrained and guided by all the checks of a representative assembly, like the British House of Commons. If one had not read it, it would be difficult to believe that a sincere believer in revealed religion could write such sheer nonsense. It is purely a question of fact, and does not admit of *à priori* reasoning. If God wished to make the

Pope an infallible interpreter of Christian faith, He can do so as easily as He sent inspired prophets in the old law, and inspired evangelists in the new; and that he did constitute the Pope the infallible teacher of His Church, we have the only testimony on which man can rationally rest his faith—the declaration of the Church of God, solemnly assembled in Council. Error in modern times assumes a thousand varied forms. It spreads with the rapidity of the lightning's flash, and is corrupting European society to its very core. The slow and cumbrous method of general councils, though efficient to check the growth of error in the past, could poorly cope with its rapid diffusion in the present. Every sincere Christian, therefore, must feel thankful to Almighty God that, in His own time, He has placed in the hands of His Vicar a two-edged sword to smite more effectively and more promptly error wherever it appears in any of its Protean forms.

As a proof of his fitness to explain to us the intrinsic nature of Papal Infallibility, Mr. Gladstone informs us that Dr. Newman will be called upon to retract the statement that "Infallibility is not inspiration". Every Catholic theologian, who ever wrote on the subject, states that Infallibility is not inspiration. Inspiration is not claimed in the bull *Unigenitus*, nor in any other bull ever issued by a Pope. It is not taught in any theologian or canonist of the Catholic Church, and is virtually disclaimed in the Vatican decree. Yet this modern Crichton coolly asserts it is the doctrine of Rome, and that Dr. Newman will be censured for holding the contrary.

Infallibility is not inspiration, and no one informed in the elementary principles of theology, could confound them. Inspiration is a divine impulse of the Holy Ghost, moving the writer, and so governing and guiding his mind, that he writes what God wishes, and the inspired writing is rightly called "vere verbum Dei". Infallibility is only an assistance which preserves the Church or the Pope from error. A definition of the Pope is not a revelation of a new doctrine, but a declaration of a doctrine formerly revealed, in which declaration the Pope is preserved from error by divine aid.

Mr. Gladstone also entertains us on the uncertainty of dogmatic decrees, as tending rather to confuse than to quiet the consciences of believers. I refer him to the words of Cardinal Manning, *Vatican Decrees*, page 29: clearer could not be written. The Pope speaks *ex cathedra* when he speaks under these five conditions:—

    1. As supreme teacher.
    2. To the whole Church.

3. Defining a doctrine.
4. To be held by the whole Church.
5. In faith and morals.

Whenever Mr. Gladstone finds all these conditions present, then he may regard the decree as dogmatic, but if even one of them is absent, then, though the pronouncement may demand his obedience as an exercise of Papal jurisdiction, it does not claim his homage as an article of faith.

CHAPTER XI.

CONCLUSION.

IN repelling the charges so freely made against our holy faith, and against the aged and venerable Pontiff, if I have used any word in the slightest degree personally offensive to Mr. Gladstone, or wanting in the respect due to his exalted character, I sincerely regret it, and can truly say that, apart from his recent publications, my feeling towards him is one of unfeigned admiration and gratitude. I regret not less the injustice he has done himself and the injury he has done the great liberal party of the Empire, than the pain his words have caused his Catholic fellow-subjects. For my part I wish to regard his present conduct as but a passing phase in the most brilliant career in the annals of English statesmen, and hope he will yet crown his great political labours by achievements still more glorious in the cause of civil, religious, and social freedom. His two great Irish measures were not as perfect as they might be, but the wonder is, not that they did not concede more to the popular demands, but that the eloquence and the genius of Mr. Gladstone was able to drag a parliament of landlords to concede so much. The perfections of the measures were due to him and to his gifted colleague, John Bright; their defects arose from the oligarchical system under which we live, and from the insincerity of some of the so-called tenant right members from Ireland. Mr. Gladstone abolished political and religious ascendency in Ireland ; and with a courage not less bold and a purpose not less pure, he endeavoured to remove that intellectual ascendency which is the most galling of our fetters and the most oppressive of our persecutions. For centuries the enlightened Christian government of England laboured to stifle the national will, to extinguish the national sentiment, to extirpate the national faith, and to brutalize the people, by debarring them from all intellectual culture, and condemning them to a forced ignorance. Under this blessed system of foreign rule, we had periodical famines which decimated the people, but we had an intellectual famine which was perpetual, and held the intellect of the country in its fell grasp, and tended to make the national mind an arid and barren wilderness. This is the system Mr. Gladstone's enemies would perpetuate, this is the system he has partially uprooted. Irishmen should not lightly forget his great services. A single act, done evidently under the influence of wounded feeling, cannot cancel our obligations of gratitude for the glorious labours of a long life devoted to our interests. If Mr. Gladstone was less earnest in his honest wish to serve Ireland, he might still be Prime Minister of England; and if, for a moment, he appears to turn from us, is it generous, is it honourable, to coquet with his opponents? For my part, even with the word of reproach on his lip, I prefer him a thousand times to his sly rival, with his blandest smile and sleekest compliment. Strong in his rectitude of purpose, ever guided by the true principle of all just legislation—the common weal, Mr. Gladstone acted boldly, but did not calculate cautiously. He sincerely wished to serve Ireland, to elevate the social position of her oppressed people, and to govern us according to Irish ideas, provided we had any ideas which could be the rule of rational government. And of his many gifts I believe not one was more nobly conceived or more generously intended than the measure which led to his overthrow.

If the University Bill was not what we expected, or what we could accept, the fault was not his, but his subalterns', who so grossly deceived him, and by their inconceivable stupidity, deprived the people of Ireland of the greatest boon ever offered them by an English minister. The Irish Catholic bishops rejected the University Bill: they had no choice in the line of action they adopted, and Mr. Gladstone should have been made aware of this. The Holy Father had condemned the principle of mixed education in Ireland as intrinsically dangerous to faith and morals. Mr. Gladstone's University Bill involved this principle in the mixed college which he proposed to found in Dublin. The bishops therefore should reject the measure, or ignore a Papal rescript on THE MOST VITAL QUESTION OF THE AGE. Mr. Gladstone placed the Irish bishops in this dilemma. Not the Irish bishops therefore, but Mr. Gladstone and his advisers, were responsible for the rejection of his Irish University Bill.

In his truly eloquent conclusion, Mr. Gladstone represents freedom and truth as the poles of Christian faith. Is there not another element of stability not less essential—authority?

We have truth revealed by the Holy Spirit, Christian liberty established by God, and authority constituted by Jesus Christ. Here is the triple phalanx which protects the Christian dispensation.

If you remove the third support—authority—which Mr. Gladstone forgot to enumerate, the whole edifice, so imposing in its grandeur, crumbles into ruins. Few men living more highly appreciate the blessings of Christian civilization than the gifted writer of *Vaticanism*, because few are so familiar with Grecian and Roman civilization, or so vividly impressed with its rottenness.

It is strange, then, that a mind so gifted, so far-seeing, should assail the great prop on which Christian civilization rests. Remove the authority of the Pope: what remains in Europe? A heterogeneous congeries of states, some in actual revolution, some thirsting for conquest, some bleeding from the wounds of recent strife, and some pale with the apprehension of impending calamities. Papal arbitration may be very distasteful to radical statesmen. Look at its substitute, the present international law of Europe. What is it but the code of the brigand and the creed of the oppressor? Remove Papal authority from the National Churches, and they soon sink down to mere human institutions, and become instruments of oppression in the hands of the State. Show me in the history of the world one national Church which preserved its independence if Papal authority was cut off or weakened. Had Gallicanism triumphed, what would the French Church be at the present day?—the mere creature of the ruling power, ready to carry out its behests, regardless of the higher functions of a Christian Church.

No wonder kings, princes, and statesmen, hate the Pope, for he alone stands between them and that absolutism for which they thirst. Bismarck, with a hellish instinct, sees this clearly; Napoleon saw it, and hence his fiendish hatred of Papal authority. Mr. Gladstone sincerely loves human liberty, restrained by Christian morality and elevated by Christian faith. It is strange he does not see that the principle of authority alone can save us from either anarchy or despotism. Constitutionalism, he will say, is our refuge. In its way it is very good, but could it survive the wreck of Christian faith, could it survive the enlightenment and sense of moral obligation which Christian faith diffuses? In a population degraded by ignorance and irreligion, what is constitutionalism but a clumsy instrument of oppression? With the present state of England before him, Mr. Gladstone's faith in constitutionalism must be sadly shaken. He gave political power to the masses, and they used it to return to office their hereditary oppressors. No—without religion and knowledge widely diffused amongst the people, constitutionalism, as the guardian of human liberty, is impossible. If you have knowledge widely diffused without religion, a constitutional government will become a communistic republic or a military despotism. If you have ignorance without religion, constitutionalism will become the parent of absolutism. Constitutionalism cannot be the permanent guardian of liberty, except in a population enlightened and religious; enlightenment and religion, widely diffused among the masses, are impossible without the aid and coöperation of the Catholic Church, which essentially rests on Papal authority.

Mr. Gladstone then, in assailing the authority of the Pope, is undermining the very foundation of human liberty, and bringing back the world as far as he can to the despotism and rottenness of Paganism. All who study the social problem must see that human liberty must rest on religion and knowledge; without the principle of authority, religion is impossible; and without religion knowledge but makes men more accomplished in wickedness and more difficult to govern. The authority of human law is the guardian of social order. The authority of human law rests on the divine, of which God's Church is constituted the legitimate interpreter. The Church speaks by the voice of her divinely constituted head— the POPE OF ROME.

THE END.

www.ingramcontent.com/pod-product-compliance
Lightning Source LLC
Chambersburg PA
CBHW032237080426
42735CB00008B/896